EXTREME PUMPKINS

Diabolical Do-It-Youself Designs to Amuse Your Friends and Scare Your Neighbors

TOM NARDONE
Creator of ExtremePumpkins.com

HOME

DEDICATION

To my wife, Lisa, who has everything except good judgment in men.

A HOME BOOK
Published by the Penguin Group
Penguin Group (USA) Inc.
375 Hudson Street, New York, New York 10014, USA

Penguin Group (Canada), 90 Eglinton Avenue East, Suite 700,
Toronto, Ontario M4P 2Y3, Canada
(a division of Pearson Penguin Canada Inc.)

Penguin Books Ltd., 80 Strand, London WC2R 0RL, England

Penguin Group Ireland, 25 St. Stephen's Green, Dublin 2, Ireland
(a division of Penguin Books Ltd.)

Penguin Group (Australia), 250 Camberwell Road, Camberwell,
Victoria 3124, Australia
(a division of Pearson Australia Group Pty. Ltd.)

Penguin Books India Pvt. Ltd., 11 Community Centre,
Panchsheel Park, New Delhi—110 017, India

Penguin Group (NZ), 67 Apollo Drive, Mairangi Bay,
Auckland 1311, New Zealand
(a division of Pearson New Zealand Ltd.)

Penguin Books (South Africa) (Pty.) Ltd., 24 Sturdee Avenue,
Rosebank, Johannesburg 2196, South Africa

Penguin Books Ltd., Registered Offices: 80 Strand,
London WC2R 0RL, England

While the author has made every effort to provide accurate telephone numbers and Internet addresses at the time of publication, neither the publisher nor the author assumes any responsibility for errors, or for changes that occur after publication. Further, the publisher does not have any control over and does not assume any responsibility for author or third-party websites or their content.

A QUIRK PACKAGING BOOK
Copyright © 2007 by Quirk Packaging, Inc.
Photography by R. Gabby Buckay and Tom Nardone
Designed by Lynne Yeamans
Edited by Sarah Scheffel
Illustrations by Nancy Leonard

First edition: September 2007

Library of Congress Cataloging-in-Publication Data

Nardone, Tom.
  Extreme pumpkins : diabolical do-it-yourself designs to amuse your friends and scare your neighbors / by Tom Nardone.
     p. cm.
  Includes index.
  ISBN 978-1-55788-522-7
  1. Halloween decorations. 2. Handicraft. I. Title.
  TT900.H32N37 2007
  745.594'1—dc22   2007002838

PRINTED IN CHINA

10   9   8   7

Most Home Books are available at special quantity discounts for bulk purchases for sales promotions, premiums, fund-raising, or educational use. Special books, or book excerpts, can also be created to fit specific needs. For details, write: Special Markets, Penguin Group (USA) Inc., 375 Hudson Street, New York, New York 10014.

DISCLAIMER

THIS BOOK IS NOT INTENDED FOR CHILDREN. The projects described in this book should be done only by adults or by older children under close adult supervision.

SAFETY FIRST: Safety should be your top priority. If you're careless, you could get injured. The publisher, author and packager of this book do not claim that the information contained herein is complete or accurate for your specific situation. It should by no means be considered a substitute for good judgment, skill, and common sense. In addition, neither the publisher, author nor packager endorses or encourages any irresponsible behavior, and specifically disclaims responsibility for any liability, loss, damage, or injury allegedly arising from any suggestion, information, or instruction in this book. We urge you to obey the law and the dictates of common sense at all times.

CONTENTS

INTRODUCTION

At some point, Halloween stopped being an outrageous, thoroughly badass holiday. Instead, in its place, we have a cutesy, warm-fuzzy event featuring friendly ghosts and waiflike witches. Even jack-o'-lanterns have lost their edge. Today's pumpkin carvers are replacing spine-chilling grimaces and horrible fangs with adorable painted renditions of popular cartoon characters. Who's scared now?

Enter *Extreme Pumpkins*, an anything-but-tame guide to pumpkin carving that will help you take back Halloween from the tame and the cheerful. You'll learn how to turn namby-pamby pumpkin carving on its head, beginning with an overview of what your extreme toolbox should contain (rev up your power tools!), outrageous design strategies (from the truly terrifying to the indisputably ridiculous), and ninja techniques, including the best way to scalp and gut a pumpkin, perform a pain-free nasal-innardectomy, and set a jack-o'-lantern bonfire. Next are instructions for carving up twenty of my favorite, thoroughly grotesque, totally pyromaniacal, or otherwise disturbing jack-o'-lanterns, including the Cannibal, Radioactive, and Mooning Pumpkins.

In exchange for sharing my extreme tricks, techniques, and tips, I have just one favor to ask of you: Promise me you will never paint adorable ghosts or "boo!" on your jack-o'-lanterns again. Instead, grab your jigsaw and your electric drill, your road flares and your kerosene-soaked toilet paper and join me in this year's great pumpkin massacre. Let's each buy a big, ugly pumpkin and carve that thing using all the power tools we own. Then let's plop these hideous pumpkins on our front porches for everyone to see. On the evening of October 31, we will light up our evil jack-o'-lanterns using whatever cheap special effects we can get our hands on.

AND HALLOWEEN WILL BE BADASS AGAIN.

THE EXTREME TOOLBOX

When it's time to carve pumpkins, I like to use power tools. They cut through pumpkin flesh like it's butter and make me feel like a brute. Below you'll find specifics about my power tool arsenal: jigsaw, reciprocating saw, router, and drill. Add a steak knife and a spoon and your extreme toolbox is complete. However, kids and teens should never use power tools without adult supervision. In fact, adults who are unfamiliar with power tools shouldn't use them without adult supervision, either.

Fortunately, power tools are not essential to creating these pumpkin designs. You can use regular hand tools and still achieve extreme results. See The Standard Toolbox: Alternatives to Power Tools, page 7.

THE JIGSAW
For Smooth Cuts and Irregular Curves

A regular kitchen knife is a poor choice if you want to carve a pumpkin in a jiffy. It's difficult to stab through the pumpkin flesh and tricky to create anything but the most obvious shapes. Beginners will only be able to make square openings with this wimpy tool. Creative types could make triangles, but circles are pretty much impossible. If you're going to create a truly expressive pumpkin, clearly you need to be able to execute a larger repertoire of geometric shapes and curves.

ENTER THE JIGSAW: This narrow, reciprocating blade is the tool of choice for making quick cuts and nice smooth curves. You can begin carving wherever you choose: eyes, ears, nose, or mouth are all good starting points. Just plunge the blade into the pumpkin flesh and pull the trigger. The barrel of the saw stays still while the saw blade goes in and out of the pumpkin so easily you'll feel as if you were cutting a lump of Jell-O.

Even the shortest jigsaw has plenty of power to slice and dice a grimace on a pumpkin, but I suggest that you get your hands on the longest blade available (mine is 8 inches [20 cm], but enough bragging).

- **FOR MAXIMUM CONTROL,** *plunge the jigsaw blade into the pumpkin before you pull the trigger to turn it on. You don' t want a runaway jigsaw wreaking havoc on your pumpkin (or your person).*

- **TO KEEP THE JIGSAW STEADY,** *I recommend holding it in position with two hands. It' s easy to overshoot your mark because the saw cuts through the pumpkin flesh so quickly; two hands will help you control the process.*

NOTE: *Handy illustrations like these of the right tools appear next to each pumpkin, so you' ll know what you need in your toolkit if you want to make that particular design.*

THE RECIPROCATING SAW
For Deep Cuts and Tough Flesh

If you are a pumpkin carver in a place like Wisconsin or Ohio, where the pumpkins (and the people) tend to be larger, you might make the reciprocating saw your weapon of choice. Unlike jigsaws, which typically have shorter blades, reciprocating saws can handle blades 10 or more inches (25 cm) long (perfect compensation for even the most profound inferiority complex). With a rapidly vibrating reciprocating saw at your command, you can slice the stem cap off even the orneriest pumpkin in a jiffy.

In fact, in my opinion, a reciprocating saw is the only adequate tool if you happen to come into possession of one of those truly humongous pumpkins. If you can carve a Christmas ham off a pig carcass with this tool (and you can), then carving a menacing face on even a jumbo, prizewinning pumpkin is a breeze with a reciprocating saw. The whole job should take you a few minutes—five max, if you're going for an elaborate expression. Reciprocating saws kick butt. They do have their limits, however....

- **REACH FOR A RECIPROCATING SAW** *when the pumpkin flesh is too thick for a jigsaw to carve with ease.*

- **RECIPROCATING SAWS ARE BIG TOOLS** *with a lot of power. This means they can be tricky to maneuver, so **A)** you may want to lift some weights before you attempt to steer one of these bad boys; and **B)** avoid your most intricate designs when you plan to use this tool. Attempt too many twists and turns and curves and you' re likely to end up with a heap of pumpkin pulp.*

THE ROUTER
For Flaying

In order to be an impressive pumpkin carver, you don't need an impressive vocabulary, but here is one term you should know. If your specialty is to strip the skin from a pumpkin patch full of pumpkins, you are an expert at flaying. That is your new word for today: "flay." You can completely flay a pumpkin or carefully remove select patches of skin—the decision is up to the flayer, and the flayer is you.

The best flaying tool is called a router. It consists of a heavy, rotating metal can mounted on a flat circular base with two handles. Used by woodworkers to round the edges of a piece of wood, it is also perfect for stripping the outer layer off a pumpkin. You can adjust the depth of the skin you remove; I usually start with the depth set at $3/8$ inch (1 cm) and make adjustments from there. Here are a few tips for novices:

- **FLAYING IS A MESSY JOB,** *and the goop can really fly. Wear safety goggles.*

- **BECAUSE A ROUTER SPINS,** *it tends to dance around a bit. Use both hands to keep it steady and work slowly.*

- **IF YOU WANT TO ACHIEVE A REALLY COOL LIGHT-ING EFFECT,** *remove only the outermost skin of the pumpkin. When you insert a high-powered light into the pumpkin cavity, it will create a warm but creepy glow through the flayed flesh.*

THE DRILL
For Perfect Holes

Sometimes your pumpkin needs a hole in his head, and an electric drill is just the right tool to create it. You could, of course, try gouging his cranium manually with a skewer or screwdriver, or stabbing it with a butcher knife, but why make him suffer? A drill is definitely the most humane method. It's also the easiest, most efficient technique for you.

- **YOU'LL WANT A SELECTION** *of drill bits so you can drill holes in a range of sizes. This will come in handy with designs like the Worm-Infested Pumpkin, page 50, where you need ample holes for the worms to crawl out of, and wee little holes for the maggots.*

- **IF YOU ARE TIRED OF DRILLING HOLES THAT ARE PERFECT AND ROUND,** *try this: after you finish drilling the hole, while your drill bit is still inside the pumpkin, wobble the drill around. That' ll make your hole look nasty and uneven.*

THE STEAK KNIFE
For Detail Work and Clean-Up Jobs

LET'S FACE IT: when you want to pop an eyeball out of a jack-o'-lantern or razor-sharpen a fang, you need something more delicate than a jigsaw. I mean, a jigsaw is perfect for carving out the eyes and mouth of your pumpkin and chopping off its stem, but when it's time to clean up your sloppy work, you'll want a knife. Because I'm a meat-and-potatoes kind of guy, I like to use a steak knife. It's thin and flexible enough to slide into any pumpkin orifice, and the serrated edges are great for extracting small chunks of pumpkin flesh. You'll find other uses for it, too:

- **WHEN TWO INCISIONS** *in your pumpkin don't meet up perfectly, or you cut a wonky circle/square/ triangle, use a steak knife to tidy them up.*

- **MY DESIGNS** *sometimes call for other vegetables, such as a parsnip Mohawk or cauliflower brains. Your handy steak knife will easily trim or chop these up.*

THE BIG SPOON
For Goop Removal

Pumpkins are full of goop. I like to use a big metal spoon to scrape the guts from the skull. The bigger the spoon, the faster the goop removal. I prefer the giant spoon that the lunch lady from the high school cafeteria used for serving. Remember her?

- **EXTREME PUMPKINS** *are not about being nice and tidy. It's okay if you leave a stringy pumpkin booger hanging from a nostril or don't scrape out every last seed. You just need to remove enough of the guts to make room for the all-important light show you'll be creating in the empty shell of your pumpkin.*

- **DON'T AUTOMATICALLY THROW AWAY** *the pumpkin guts. Sometimes they are key to a design; see Puking Pumpkin, page 46.*

THE STANDARD TOOLBOX
ALTERNATIVES TO POWER TOOLS

You don't have to use power tools to create the twenty extreme pumpkins in this book. You can achieve extremely cool results with hand tools, too. You only need a few items in your toolkit: here's the scoop.

PUMPKIN-CARVING TOOLS (For Smooth Cuts and Irregular Curves): **Instead of a jigsaw, use a saw from a standard pumpkin-carving kit to carve your pumpkin's face. It's not as fast, but you can get wicked results.**

DRYWALL SAW (For Deep Cuts and Tough Flesh): **Instead of a reciprocating saw, use a drywall saw to carve super-sized pumpkins. This short, stiff-bladed saw is also good for scalping pumpkins. Pick one up at any hardware store or home center.**

CARVING CHISEL (For Flaying): **Instead of a router, pick up a carving chisel at your neighborhood hardware store. The sharp metal blade of this little hand tool is good for flaying the skin off your pumpkin, whether you want to remove small patches or skin the entire thing.**

You will also need a STEAK KNIFE, for clean-up jobs and detail work, and a BIG METAL SPOON, to scoop out all the nasty goop.

RENEGADE DESIGN STRATEGIES

I can't tell you how many times I have heard some variation of the following: "How in the world did you think of that disgusting/ridiculous/terrifying/extremely cool pumpkin design?" Usually, this is followed by: "You must be a truly violent/gross/very hip person." And it sometimes finishes with "crazy bastard!"

When I first think of any new jack-o'-lantern design, I make sure it meets the following criteria before I place it with pride on my porch. To be considered genuinely extreme, a pumpkin has to possess at least one of the following qualities. It must be 1) extremely gross, 2) truly terrifying, 3) genuinely funny, or 4) undeniably cool. The twenty pumpkins in this book are all certifiably extreme; the best designs embody more than one of these virtues. Here's how to put your own pumpkin designs to the test. Ask yourself:

IS IT EXTREMELY GROSS?

Trying to decide if something is truly gross is easy. Casually mention your design idea to some friends and see if they say, "Awwww, gross!" If they do, good job. If no one uses "gross" or synonyms like "disgusting" or "revolting," then back to the drawing board you go. Remember: Your larger goal is to scare off greedy kids who want to eat all your Halloween candy. If you can make them lose their appetite, you win.

IS IT TRULY TERRIFYING?

I recently saw a pumpkin at the supermarket. It was decorated with a painted-on ghost. The ghost was white and wearing a black top hat and a smile. It had a caption that read "Happy Halloween." This, my friends, is not frightening at all. My credit card balance is more terrifying than a ghost with a top hat. Old age is scary. Impotence is frightening. And the IRS is the most terrifying organization in the country. Forget about Casper the Friendly Ghost; come up with something that really makes the hair stand up on the back of your neck.

IS IT GENUINELY FUNNY?

A truly funny pumpkin is probably the most difficult to achieve of all. You see, humor is found in the unexpected. After someone has seen something even once, it's no longer unexpected and, hence, no longer funny. If you are going to attempt to achieve the funny factor, try not to tell anyone about your design before you put it out on your porch on Halloween night. You'll preserve the surprise and the humor along with it.

IS IT UNDENIABLY COOL?

This can be tricky. For instance, I bet you think that carving the name of a rock band on your pumpkin would be badass. So did my cousin Dave . . . back in 1986. His pumpkin read "Quiet Riot." Two words: not cool. Your favorite character from a movie, TV show, or sci-fi book is not universally accepted as cool, either, but if you work at it, you can come up with a pumpkin design so completely original and out-there that it'll make even the so-hip-it-hurts crowd say, ". . . wow."

NINJA PUMPKIN-CARVING TECHNIQUES

Whether you are making one of the extreme pumpkins envisioned by my sick little brain or creating a completely original design of your own, here is an overview of the "how-to" techniques every extreme pumpkin-carver must master.

HOW TO SCALP A PUMPKIN AND OTHER RUDE PROCEDURES

It's much easier to carve a pumpkin after you've removed all the membranes and seeds. Here are two equally good methods for accessing the goop:

Basic Scalp Job

It's not easy to scalp a pumpkin. Choose a reciprocating saw with a long blade for this job.

1. **PIERCE** the pumpkin a few inches from its stem.

2. Carefully **CUT** a circle around its stem. **SWING** the handle of the saw in an arc larger than the blade as you go. This should carve out a cone-shaped plug.

3. **PULL OUT** the plug. Congratulations, you have **SCALPED** your first pumpkin.

4. **GUT** your pumpkin, using a big metal spoon to scrape out the innards and remove all the goop.

Nasal-Innardectomy

One day, I was wiping my son's very snotty, runny nose when I had an "ah-ha" moment. It occurred to me that there might be more than one exit for the removal of pumpkin guts. In fact, any large orifice will do.

1. **CARVE** your pumpkin's face. Make sure you create at least one opening that's large enough to accommodate easy goop removal.

2. **GUT** your pumpkin using a big metal spoon to pick your pumpkin's nose or yank the goop out of its eye sockets and mouth.

BEST PRACTICES

HOW TO GUT A PUMPKIN

Whether you scalp your pumpkin or perform a nasal-innardectomy, here are tips on how to most efficiently remove the goop.

- Use a long, steel-handled spoon with a sharp metal tip that'll slice quickly through the pumpkin flesh and goop.

- If you're the thrifty type and have no problem eating stuff that came out of your pumpkin's nose, separate the seeds from the goop. Roast them according to the directions on page 61.

FRANKENSTEIN'S WORKSHOP

HOW TO MAKE FAKE BLOOD

Making your own phony blood is fun and inexpensive. It requires only four ingredients and the resulting blood looks real, is safe to eat, and, when stored in a sealed container, stays fresh for months. I'll bet my house that you already have all the ingredients and tools in your kitchen. The only downside: just like real blood, fake blood attracts flies. Wait until Halloween night to use it.

YOU'LL NEED

- 1 tablespoon (8g) cornstarch
- ½ cup (125 ml) corn syrup
- ¼ cup (60 ml) cold water
- Red food coloring (about 10 drops)
- Blue food coloring (as necessary)
- 1 microwave-safe container
- 1 spoon, fork, or stick

1) Put the cornstarch in a microwave-safe container and pour in a little bit of corn syrup (about a third of it).

2) Mix the cornstarch and corn syrup with the spoon/fork/stick until you get a cementlike mixture. Then add the rest of the corn syrup. Keep stirring to thoroughly mix in the cornstarch. (I know it sounds persnickety to add a little corn syrup and then the rest of the corn syrup but adding it in two stages prevents lumps.)

3) Add the food coloring, starting with red and adjusting with blue as needed, until you get the shade that you want. A little goes a long way. I use about ten drops and it looks cool.

4) Cover the container and microwave on high for a couple of minutes. Everyone's microwave is different, but you want the mixture to boil.

5) Remove from microwave, stir, and let cool. Pour the blood into a squeeze bottle for easy application.

AWESOME SPECIAL EFFECTS

I was in the Boy Scouts for years. Let me tell you something about the Boy Scouts: It was a tough organization. The older kids made you do their chores, the scoutmaster wanted you to be neat and orderly, and Mother Nature was completely unpredictable. We seemed to be rained on every time we went camping. I stuck with it, though. Impressed? You shouldn't be. I just wanted to learn how to start fires.

Over the years, my fascination with fires has only grown. I have never been content lighting my pumpkins with a candle or a flashlight. I want flames, giant flames—the bigger the better. And because you're reading this book, I'm going to assume that you do, too. On the following pages, you'll find a must-have guide to creating awesome fires.

Beware: HERE'S WHAT CAN GO WRONG WHEN MIXING A BLOODBATH.

- If the mixture is too thin, mix up another pot of paste and add it to the tub.

- Don't try to add raw flour to the tub; it will just make lumps.

- Rinse the pot as soon as you empty it. Otherwise, your paste will dry in the pot, and your wife may never forgive you.

BLOODY MARY
HOW TO MAKE YOUR OWN BLOOD BATH

Nothing says "I'm a little bit creepy" like a bathtub full of fake blood. This recipe produces thick, red blood that anyone who's a little creepy will love.

YOU'LL NEED
- **6 cups** *(750 g)* **flour**
- **Hot water**
- **Red food coloring**
- **Blue food coloring** *(optional)*
- **The biggest pot you own**
- **Bathtub**

1) Place the flour in a big, big pot. Add a couple cups of hot water.

2) Stir until you have a flour-water paste. Once the paste is nice and smooth, add a bit more water to the pot.

3) Bring to a boil and cook for 5 minutes, then let this pasty liquid cool.

4) Fill a bathtub with hot water and add your pot of paste. Add enough red food coloring to get the color just how you like it.

5) If the mixture looks too cherry red, add a small amount of blue food coloring.

Kerosene

For Killer Flames and Dark, Stinky Smoke

Who knew that the Boy Scouts would actually teach me something useful? I learned that a toilet paper roll soaked in kerosene will create flames three feet (1 m) high. This ultra-impressive bonfire lasts a glorious forty-five minutes or so. Kerosene is available at almost every hardware store in the country, so go get some. Be careful where you light that thing, though. Indoors is definitely a no-go, and lighting up on the porch could result in some real trouble. For step-by-step directions and tips on how to avoid singeing your nose hairs, see page 21.

Charcoal Lighter Fluid

For Less Smoky Flames

For a little less smoke, use charcoal lighter fluid. Soaking a roll of toilet paper with the stuff is good, but so is filling the pumpkin with crinkled up newspaper, sprinkling with fluid, and lighting that. The newspaper won't burn as long, but it does engulf the entire inside of the pumpkin with flame. And that makes for a great photo op. See page 21 for everything you need to know.

Glow Sticks

For a Creepy Glow

When I make a nuclear waste pumpkin, I feel strongly that it should emit a strange green glow. To do this, snap a bunch of glow sticks so that they start glowing and then use a pair of heavy-duty scissors or garden sheers to open them. Most glow sticks are nontoxic, which, when you think about it, is probably a good idea. However, I have a feeling you won't win any court cases if you hurt yourself after willingly opening up a glow stick with a pair of scissors, so check the labels carefully to be sure you have the nontoxic kind. Insert the glow sticks in your jack-o'-lantern and stand back to watch the fallout. For more complete instructions and a photo, see the Radioactive Pumpkin, page 66.

Flares

For Visible-for-Miles Flames

If you want people to be able to see your pumpkin a mile up the road, use a road flare. They are awesome. Besides their awesome, red glow, they also have a cool sulfur smell that conjures up my vision of hell. Plus, they're so bright, they not only beam through the eyes and other orifices of your pumpkin, you can see their glow right through the pumpkin flesh.

You can buy road flares at an automotive or hardware store. They aren't free, but for fifteen minutes of fame, you will be a rock star. **A NOTE OF CAUTION:** Don't hold on to a road flare for very long. Instead, cut a hole in the back of the pumpkin, insert the flare, and strike up.

HOW TO PRESERVE YOUR PUMPKIN

I have heard of all sorts of methods for preserving pumpkin designs, from deep-freezing them to completely coating their surfaces in petroleum jelly. If you are desperate enough to fill your entire deep-freeze with a giant jack-o'-lantern, allow me to recommend a simpler method of preservation. Simply spray any cut surface with WD-40, that magical product usually used to stop rusty hinges from squeaking. Once the WD-40 is on the flesh, it spreads to a thin layer that triples the life of your pumpkin by delaying the onset of rot; just wait thirty minutes before lighting your jack-o'-lantern on fire. More good news: bugs, birds, and squirrels all seem to think WD-40 tastes terrible. Don't say I never taught you something useful.

A FEW WORDS ON SAFETY

Reading something that I wrote about safety is like reading something Jenna Jameson wrote about celibacy. Mmmm . . . Jenna Jameson. Oh, right! Let's get back to safety. Here are ten safety rules that, if followed, should allow you to carve pumpkins using power tools without losing even a single limb.

1) Don't be a dumbass.

2) You know that part of the jigsaw or reciprocating saw that moves? Don't touch it if the saw is plugged in.

3) Oh, yeah, and don't touch the saw blade if it's moving.

4) Don't ever put a pumpkin on your lap to carve it.

5) If you need to burn stuff, always do it outside.

6) Don't light anything on fire if you have any residue of it on your person or clothes.

7) A garden hose won't put out a kerosene fire. You need a fire extinguisher for that (type A-B or A-B-C—be sure to follow the manufacturer's instructions).

8) If you have to lift something heavy (like a really big pumpkin or your couch), trick your friends into doing it for you.

9) Sharp things can poke and cut you. So, pay attention.

10) If blood starts coming out of you (and it isn't my fake recipe), take immediate action. A little pressure and a bandage should do the job; a lot and you need to get yourself to the emergency room.

That about sums it up. If you can abide by rule number one, you should do okay . . . assuming we share the same definition of dumbass.

CANNIBAL PUMPKIN

LIFE REQUIRES BRAVERY; if you're timid, the cannibals will eat you for sure. To illustrate this point, each year I buy a giant pumpkin and feed other pumpkins to it. A ruthless jack-o'-lantern munching on the flesh of its own kind really frightens all the sweater-vest types. Here's how you can scare your neighbors, too.

At Night in the Pumpkin Patch, the Big Eat the Little

YOU'LL NEED

- **1 giant pumpkin** *(50 to 100 pounds [23 to 45 kg] would be awe-inspiring)*

- **1 small pumpkin** *(about one-fourth the height of your giant pumpkin)*

- **CARVING AND GUTTING TOOLS: jigsaw, reciprocating saw** *(if pumpkin flesh is tough)*, **router** *(to shave off pumpkin skin)*, **steak knife, big metal spoon**

  NOTE: Power tools are optional. *(See The Standard Toolbox: Alternatives to Power Tools, page 7.)*

- **Dry erase marker**

- **WD-40**

1. **CUT** a face in the smaller "victim" pumpkin and **SCOOP** out excess flesh. Go for a pathetic expression. If you were being eaten alive, you'd look pathetic, too.

2. **TRACE** the smaller pumpkin, holding it up to one side of where the giant cannibal pumpkin's mouth will be carved.

3 **CUT** a hole in the giant pumpkin a little bit smaller than the widest part of the small pumpkin. Remember, you can always cut a hole larger, but it is very tough to cut a hole smaller.

4 **SKETCH** the rest of the cannibal's mouth. Try to make it look like the mouth is closing in on the smaller, victim pumpkin. Turn up the corners of the giant pumpkin's mouth for a sinister look.

5 **GUT** the cannibal pumpkin. You might need your entire arsenal of tools for this job: jigsaw, reciprocating saw, router, and spoon.

6 **DRAW** the cannibal pumpkin an angry set of eyes and nose. A furrowed brow and a pointed nose (possibly made from a chunk of another pumpkin) look menacing.

7 **CARVE** the eyes, nose, and mouth, including some big, nasty teeth. **SHAVE** the pumpkin skin off the eyeballs and teeth so they look especially 3D and vicious.

8 **JAM** the small pumpkin into the mouth of the cannibal pumpkin. It should be a tight fit. If the opening is too small, **SCRAPE** the edges to make room.

9 **SPRAY** the cut or gutted surfaces of both pumpkins with WD-40 to preserve them. They should last for a week or so before they rot.

WASTE MANAGEMENT

HOW TO DISPOSE OF A GIANT PUMPKIN CARCASS

Sure, it may have seemed like a great idea to buy a monstrous pumpkin and watch your neighbors gape at that sucker on your front porch. But now you have a week or two to get rid of that thing before it rots, and damn, is it heavy.

Before your neighbors report you to the sanitation department, follow these waste management tips, which a wise and compassionate pumpkin farmer shared with me. To remove the pumpkin carcass from your porch, roll it onto a beach towel and ask a buddy to grab the other two corners of the towel. Waddle downstairs and heave the carcass onto the grass, near the curb. Using an axe, hack the flesh into watermelon-sized chunks. Place them in the sturdiest trash bags you can find—I recommend those high-capacity versions designed for hard use, such as contractor or lawn and leaf bags. To sidestep a potential mess, one chunk of flesh per bag is best. To avoid attracting vermin, seal tightly. If the trash man won't pick them up, you can always redeposit the bags in your neighbor's garbage cans in the dead of night.

"MY HEAD IS ON FIRE" PUMPKIN

NOT TOO MANY HALLOWEENS PAST, I was enjoying the effects of a fully lit jack-o'-lantern when I suddenly thought, "Hey, why does that idiot have a grin on his face? I mean, his head is on fire. That's gotta hurt like hell." This insight led me to create the "My Head Is on Fire" Pumpkin, featuring an appropriately agonized expression and a spiky, flame-shaped crown.

And You Thought You Were Having a Bad Day...

BURN, BABY, BURN

HOW TO CREATE A BONFIRE IN YOUR JACK-O'-LANTERN

If you want a large, scenic fire that will die down quickly (i.e., before your front porch catches on fire), use CHARCOAL LIGHTER FLUID. I crinkle up newspaper, put the paper inside the pumpkin cavity, and then soak it with lighter fluid. The flames last for a dazzling minute or two.

If you want a large, long-lasting fire and you don't mind some black smoke, then you should soak a roll of toilet paper in KEROSENE, insert it in the cavity of your pumpkin (make sure there is air space around it), and light it. Through this method, you can achieve three-foot-high flames that last for forty-five minutes. How cool is that? Your neighbors will appoint you the God of Halloween.

YOU'LL NEED

- **1 pumpkin shaped like a human head and roomy enough to easily fit a roll of toilet paper inside**

- **Dry erase marker**

- **CARVING AND GUTTING TOOLS: jigsaw, reciprocating saw** (if pumpkin flesh is tough), **steak knife, big metal spoon**

  NOTE: Power tools are optional. (See The Standard Toolbox: Alternatives to Power Tools, page 7.)

FOR CHARCOAL LIGHTER FLUID FIRE:

- **Dry newspaper**

- **Charcoal lighter fluid** (I buy the cheapest stuff possible)

FOR KEROSENE FIRE:

- **Bucket** (to soak the toilet paper)

- **Kerosene** (available at the hardware store and even some gas stations)

- **Roll of toilet paper**

- **Long lighter or long kitchen matches**

- **Fire extinguisher** (type A-B or A-B-C)

- **Camera** (optional, but I bet you'll want a photo of this)

1. **DRAW** a pained expression on the pumpkin. Eyes that look upward will emphasize its anguish.

2. **SKETCH** a crown of flames encircling the pumpkin's head. Don't get too fancy because you're going to have to carve what you've sketched.

3. **SCALP** and **GUT** the pumpkin.

4. **CARVE** the face and flames in the pumpkin. **CLEAN** rough edges.

5. **CUT** a few vent holes (each about 2 inches [5 cm] wide) in the backside of the pumpkin about one-third of the way up. These vents will feed air to the fire.

6. **GO OUTSIDE** and position the pumpkin far away from anything flammable. If your lawn is dry, spray it down with the hose before you light the pumpkin.

7. If you are using the charcoal lighter fluid method, stuff **CRUMPLED** newspaper in the pumpkin cavity and **DRENCH** it with the lighter fluid. If you are using the kerosene method, **SOAK** the toilet paper in the kerosene for at least 30 minutes. **INSERT** the toilet paper into the pumpkin cavity.

8. **CALL** your neighbors and invite them to come over and enjoy your mini bonfire. Give the fire extinguisher to the most responsible person present.

9. **LIGHT** the flammables through the mouth. (Lighting the pumpkin from the top is a surefire way to burn your hand.)

10. **STEP BACK** and **ENJOY** the show. Take a picture; it'll last longer.

THREE HAIKU
INSPIRED BY THIS PUMPKIN

Flames lick three feet high,
Scaring neighborhood children.
More candy left for me.

Fire Marshal Kenny
Gave me a ticket tonight.
No guts, no glory.

Pumpkin burning bright.
Kerosene lights the front porch.
Neighbors freak. I laugh.

Beware: Don't light up this (or any) jack-o'-lantern inside your home or without adult supervision. If the flames even threaten to become out of control, use your fire extinguisher. If that doesn't put out the fire immediately, call 911.

PROPERTY-DEFENDER
PUMPKIN

ONE OF MY MOST ELABORATE DESIGNS, this vengeful pumpkin has slain all the other pumpkins and stands triumphant atop the heap, with pumpkin guts dripping from his hands and an unapologetic smirk on his face. You may be a peace-loving type, but if you've ever been pushed too far, this pumpkin is for you. In fact, it may be your self-portrait.

No Guts, No Glory

YOU'LL NEED

- **3 pumpkins, each one larger than the next** (the smallest should be the size of a human head; the largest should be the size of a big potbelly)

- **CARVING AND GUTTING TOOLS: jigsaw, reciprocating saw** (if pumpkin flesh is tough), **router** (to shave off pumpkin skin), **steak knife, big metal spoon**

  NOTE: Power tools are optional. (See The Standard Toolbox: Alternatives to Power Tools, page 7.)

- **2 forked sticks** (these should resemble arms with hands on the ends)

- **2 long stakes** (4-foot [1.2 m] pieces of 2 x 2-inch [5 x 5 cm] lumber will do the trick)

- **Reciprocating saw** (for sharpening the stakes); **mallet, hammer, or sledgehammer** (for pounding them into your lawn)

- **A variety of smashed pumpkins** (either gather these from the neighborhood or smash up your own)

- **Spotlight or strobe** (optional)

1. **CARVE** an angry face on the smallest pumpkin. Give it an open, menacing mouth. **GUT** it through the mouth and **CLEAN** rough edges.

2. **CUT** two armholes in the medium-sized pumpkin. I used a router to **SHAVE** buttons (or battle scars) off the pumpkin's chest.

3. **ARRANGE** the three pumpkins as you would a snowman. That is, the largest pumpkin should be on the bottom of the pile; the smallest should be on top.

4. **CUT** two 2-inch (5 cm) holes in the top and bottom of each pumpkin, about 4 inches (10 cm) apart. Take care to keep the pumpkins in alignment.

5. **SHARPEN** the stakes and **DRIVE** them into the ground, approximately 4 inches (10 cm) apart. Test them to make sure they are stable.

6 **MOUNT** the pumpkins on the stakes, piling them on top of one another. **SAW** off the ends of the stakes if they're too long.

7 **INSERT** the forked sticks in the medium-sized pumpkin to create arms.

8 **ARRANGE** the smashed pumpkins around the base of the your vengeful Property Defender. For maximum effect, place some pumpkin guts in its hands and mouth.

9 **ILLUMINATE** your creation from below, if desired.

PUMPKIN CARNAGE SCENES

YOU CAN BUILD IN YOUR FRONT YARD

If you've got an active (meaning twisted) imagination, you might enjoy constructing one of these large-scale scenes of jack-o'-lantern mayhem. If you're handy, any of these scenarios could be constructed using cast-off items from around the house. I'll admit, they're ambitious, but what do you really have to do this weekend anyway?

- A pumpkin funeral

- A pumpkin autopsy

- Frankenstein's monster, pumpkin style

- A pumpkin car crash with horrified pumpkin

- A mourning pumpkin crying as it looks at a smashed pumpkin

- A horrified pumpkin roasted on your barbecue grill

- A gathering of pumpkins feasting on a butternut squash

- Pumpkins impaled upon your picket fence

- The top half of a pumpkin drowning in your birdbath

- A pumpkin run over by your lawnmower or impaled with your garden tools

BRAIN-SURGERY PUMPKIN

NOTHING GIVES PEOPLE THE HEEBIE-JEEBIES LIKE BRAINS. In fact, most people would prefer to witness a still-beating heart than the spilling of human gray matter. That is what gives this extreme pumpkin its gross-out power: People are simultaneously repulsed by the brains bursting from its severed cranium and fascinated by their construction. Many will want to touch the oozing innards to see what they're made of, but most will pull back in disgust.

They Say He's Changed Since the Experiment

YOU'LL NEED

- **Dry erase marker**

- **1 pumpkin, any shape** *(its diameter should be 8 or 9 inches [20 or 23 cm], about the size of a pie plate)*

- **CARVING AND GUTTING TOOLS: jigsaw, reciprocating saw** *(if pumpkin flesh is tough),* **steak knife, big metal spoon**

  NOTE: Power tools are optional. *(See The Standard Toolbox: Alternatives to Power Tools, page 7.)*

- **Aluminum foil pie plate**

- **1 can of Great Stuff** *(or other cream-colored expanding foam insulation)*

- **Pair of old or disposable gloves**

1 **DRAW** a horrified face on the lower two-thirds of your pumpkin. Try to come up with a convincing expression of genuine agony, such as a gaping, down-turned mouth and droopy eyes.

2 **SCALP** the pumpkin, removing the top one-fourth of the head to reveal a gaping hole where the pie plate will fit snugly. (The pie plate will serve as the "brainpan.")

3 **GUT** the pumpkin and **CARVE** its face. **CLEAN** rough edges.

4 **INSERT** the pie plate in the opening, right side up, to block it off and support the brains. Without the pie plate, you would have to fill the entire pumpkin with insulation, which would be a big waste of Great Stuff.

5 Following the instructions on the can of Great Stuff, **FILL** the pie plate with the insulation. **WEAR** gloves because that stuff is about the stickiest thing I've ever encountered. The human brain is made out of a left and right lobe; why not take an extra five seconds to make your brains look as realistic as possible?

6 **WALK AWAY.** The foam will expand as it hardens leaving you with a mighty cool pumpkin. Let it dry for at least 1 hour before you put it out on your porch. After your pumpkin rots, you can stash the brain for next year.

MIND GAMES

BRAINY FACTS FOR BRAINY FOLKS

- It may be powerful, but your brain represents only about 2 percent of your entire bodyweight. To put this in perspective:

  - An adult human brain weighs around 3 pounds.

  - An elephant brain weighs more than 12 pounds.

  - Starfish have no centralized brain at all.

- An amazing 80 percent of your brain is water.

- Your brain continues to produce new cells during your adult life, a process known as neurogenesis.

- Of all the oxygen you breathe, 20 percent fuels your brain activity.

- Impulses to and from the brain travel as fast as

- People who ride roller coasters regularly are much more likely to have a blood clot affect their brain. But don't let me ruin your fun . . .

- Despite our impressions to the contrary, your brain thinks more at night than during the day.

- The idea that 90 percent of our brainpower is unused is not based on any scientific fact. Psychic types like to keep this myth going because they want to believe that our brains have excess capacity. (Of course these folks get $80 an hour to use their excess capacity to read our minds.)

- The inside of the skull where the brain is stored is pink in color due to the blood flowing through it.

ROADKILL–EATING PUMPKIN

THE ROADKILL-EATING PUMPKIN IS A BY-PRODUCT OF THE MOST GRUESOME EVENT I've ever been involved in. Bambi jumped out of the woods just in time to get its head stuck between my pickup's front wheel and the lip of the fender. Luckily, a cop helped me haul the bloody carcass into the woods. Before doing so, he asked, "Do you want to keep it? It's a legal kill, you know. You can eat it." I looked at Bambi, whose head was almost completely severed, and politely declined.

Expect a Phone Call from Your Block Committee

YOU'LL NEED

- **Dry erase marker**

- **1 big, ugly pumpkin** *(25 pounds [11.5 kg] minimum but the bigger, the cooler)*

- **CARVING AND GUTTING TOOLS: jigsaw, reciprocating saw** *(if pumpkin flesh is tough)*, **router** *(to shave off pumpkin skin)*, **steak knife, big metal spoon**

  NOTE: Power tools are optional. *(See The Standard Toolbox: Alternatives to Power Tools, page 7.)*

- **A stuffed animal that you don't mind destroying**

- **Black tape** *(optional)*

- **Fake blood** *(see page 10 for recipe)*

1. **DRAW** a mean face on the pumpkin. Give it big, intimidating teeth.

2. **SCALP** and **GUT** the pumpkin.

3. **CARVE** the pumpkin's face. If you want big, yellow, cruel-looking eyeballs, **SHAVE** off the pumpkin skin.

4. **SLICE** open the abdomen of your stuffed animal and **DISCARD** most of the stuffing. This should leave it looking limp and lifeless.

5 COVER the eyes of the stuffed animal with Xs made from the black tape, if you want. In the world of cartoons, Xs are the universal symbol that a creature has died a tragic yet somehow oddly humorous death.

6 POUR the fake blood and optional chicken gizzards all over the scene of the crime. This will look incredibly gory.

7 POSITION the stuffed animal so that it hangs dramatically from the pumpkin's jaws.

8 DRIZZLE WITH more blood so it's dripping from the corners of the pumpkin's mouth. Any creature that eats roadkill will certainly not be neat about it.

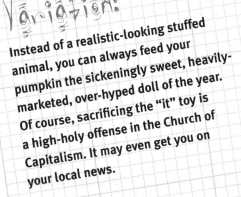

Variation:

Instead of a realistic-looking stuffed animal, you can always feed your pumpkin the sickeningly sweet, heavily-marketed, over-hyped doll of the year. Of course, sacrificing the "it" toy is a high-holy offense in the Church of Capitalism. It may even get you on your local news.

ROADKILL STATISTICS

Want to know how many cute, defenseless critters have been mangled under car wheels lately? It's estimated that about a million animals die each day on U.S. roads. Working with data collected by students in New England, *Animal People* newspaper came up with these extrapolated numbers of creatures killed annually:

- 41 million squirrels
- 26 million cats
- 22 million rats
- 19 million opossums
- 15 million raccoons
- 6 million dogs
- 350,000 deer
- 5,412 human pedestrians

To give you a little perspective, that would mean you have a one in a thousand chance of killing a deer this year. And a squirrel? I'd be surprised if you didn't knock one off while driving home today.

ELECTROCUTED PUMPKIN

MY INTERPRETATION OF WHAT AN ELECTROCUTION LOOKS LIKE may be a little lacking in realism, but this pumpkin still draws crowds. The key is wattage: This jack-o'-lantern is lit up with a road flare, and those things can be seen from half a mile away. I may not be a master carver, but darned if I don't use more power than anyone else. You, too, can dazzle your neighbors through cheap pyrotechnics: Turn the page for step-by-step directions.

Blowdrying your hair while you're in the bathtub? Add it to your list of very bad ideas.

(1) **CUT** an array of tall, slender triangles circling the top third of your pumpkin. These will be the jack-o'-lantern's spiked hair; they also look a little like flames, which seems appropriate. **PULL OFF** the top of the pumpkin, including the stem, and discard it.

(2) **GUT** the pumpkin.

(3) **CARVE** a shocked-looking face. I use stars for the eyes, but you could use a lightning bolts or whatever shape works for you. **CLEAN** rough edges.

(4) **PUT** your pumpkin on the porch and stick an (unlit) road flare in it.

(5) **WATCH TV** or otherwise occupy yourself until nightfall. Then strike up your flare (be sure to light it through an eyehole, not the top of the head) and enjoy the spectacle.

BEWARE: If your road flare is flaring longer than you want it to, you can extinguish it against the side of your pumpkin. Wear gloves and be sure to grasp the stick through the mouth (not the crown!) of the pumpkin.

YOU'LL NEED

- **1 pumpkin shaped like a human head** *(any size will do)*

- **CARVING AND GUTTING TOOLS: jigsaw, steak knife, big metal spoon**

  NOTE: Power tools are optional. *(See The Standard Toolbox: Alternatives to Power Tools, page 7.)*

- **1 road flare** *(available at your local auto parts store)*

- **Fire extinguisher** *(type A-B or A-B-C)*

- The word *electrocution* did not exist until after 1887, the year the state of New York held a competition to come up with a name for their new method of execution, considered to be more humane than hanging.

- Runner-up names were "electromort" and "electricide." (Note: Do not confuse "electricide" with the "electric slide," an awful line dance done at bad weddings and sixteen-year-olds' birthday parties.)

- Nikola Tesla presented his idea for the AC generator to Thomas Edison. When Edison refused to help with the project, Tesla went to George Westinghouse for support. Edison started a campaign against AC power, claiming that it was much more dangerous than DC power. To prove his point, he set up public demonstrations where he electrocuted dogs and cats using AC power. He also convinced the authorities at Sing Sing to carry out death sentences by electrocution.

- The first excecution using AC power didn't go well. Instead of killing the man immediately, he was almost cooked, filling the air with the smell of burning flesh.

- Amnesty International reported that the cycle in one execution was 1,825 volts at 7.5 amps for 30 seconds followed by 240 volts for 60 seconds. Supposedly, this first rendered the brain dead and next stopped the remaining organs.

- Approximately 400 people die in the U.S. from accidental electrocutions each year. Eleven percent of those people are electrocuted while working with household wiring.

PUNK ROCK PUNKIN

I USED TO FANCY MYSELF A PUNK ROCK KID.

I had a Mohawk, a black leather jacket, and steel-toed boots. When Black Flag's Henry Rollins sang "Rise Above," I screamed along as if I had written the anthem myself. For two-and-a-half adrenaline-pounding minutes, I believed I was the real deal, but I didn't fool my parents or even my dog. As a tribute to those rebellious days, I created this flat-black pumpkin and the Mohawk-sporting variation on page 41. God save the Queen!

Never Mind the Bollocks, I'm a Punkin

YOU'LL NEED

- **1 pimply-textured pumpkin** (choose one twice the size of a human head)

- **1 large cardboard box** (optional)

- **1 can flat-black spray paint**

- **CARVING AND GUTTING TOOLS:**
  jigsaw or reciprocating saw
  (if pumpkin flesh is tough),
  steak knife, big metal spoon

  NOTE: Power tools are optional.
  (See The Standard Toolbox:
  Alternatives to Power Tools, page 7.)

- **Staple gun**

- **Staples, rings, safety pins**
  (or whatever else you want to use
  to pierce your pumpkin)

- **A selection of carrots and parsnips**
  for Mohawk (optional)

- **Strobe light or road flare** (optional)

- **Fire extinguisher** (type A-B or A-B-C)

1. **BUILD** a temporary spray-painting booth by cutting off two sides of the cardboard box. If you don't want to bother with the cardboard, just spray paint the pumpkin on the grass. In five weeks, you'll forget that you ever painted the lawn black.

2. **SPRAY PAINT** a section of the pumpkin, rotate it, and spray paint the next section, until the entire pumpkin is coated in black, even the stem. If you want, add another layer of paint after the first one dries to make the pumpkin to look as ominous as possible.

3. **IMAGINE** the grimace of your favorite punk rocker: Sid Vicious, Keith Morris, Siouxsie Sioux, Billy Joe Armstrong—the choice is yours. Now **CARVE** the pumpkin's face in that likeness. **CLEAN** the rough edges.

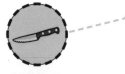

4) **GUT** your pumpkin through the eyes or nose or mouth—any orifice will do.

5) **PIERCE** your pumpkin using the staple gun and whatever hardware you scrounged up.

6) If you want your punkin to have a Mohawk, **CUT** a row of slightly undersized holes in its crown. Shove the carrots and parsnips through the holes from the inside of the pumpkin.

7) **LIGHT** your punkin with a strobe light and it will look really cool. Of course, a road flare is pretty badass, too. Its glow only lasts 15 minutes, but when you think about it, that's longer than most punk albums.

PUNK ROCK PLAYLIST
FOR PUMPKIN CARVERS

It's a free country. You're welcome to listen to whatever you want while you hack up your pumpkins, but I recommend punk rock. Here's a list of ten tunes guaranteed to get you in the mood for carving time.

1) "London Calling," The Clash
2) "I Wanna Be Sedated," The Ramones
3) "Kick Out the Jams," MC5
4) "Search and Destroy," Iggy and the Stooges
5) "Straight Edge," Minor Threat
6) "Rise Above," Black Flag
7) "Where Eagles Dare," Misfits
8) "Los Angeles," X
9) "Anarchy in the UK," The Sex Pistols
10) "Longview," Greenday

BURGER PUMPKIN

TRANSFORMING A PUMPKIN INTO A GIANT BURGER BUN IS FUN AND STRANGE; it will win any office-sponsored pumpkin-carving contest because fun and strange is what groups of bored people stuck in an office building enjoy. Besides, what's more crowd-pleasing than burgers? At my office, we've had competitions to see who could down a Quadruple Whopper, a king-sized order of fries, and a 44-ounce (1.4 l) soda the fastest. The whole meal was 2,460 calories and weighed $3\frac{1}{2}$ pounds (1.5 kg). The winner came in at a little over eight minutes. Even if you're not stupid enough to engage in such a contest, you can make this supersized homage to the burger.

Warning: This Pumpkin Is a Magnet for Neighborhood Dogs (and Hungry Mailmen)

YOU'LL NEED

- **1 pumpkin** (*about the size of a cantaloupe and vaguely shaped like a burger bun*)

- **CARVING AND GUTTING TOOLS: handsaw and a big metal spoon**

- **Paper towels**

- **2¹/₂ pounds** (*1 kg*) **ground beef**

- **Stove, big skillet, cooking oil, and a platter bigger than your skillet**

- **Oven mitts**

- **Lettuce, tomatoes, pickles, and whatever other toppings you like**

- **Glue**

1. **CUT** the pumpkin in half from top to bottom through the stem end. A handsaw will do the trick. If you try to use a carving knife, you will have a tough time.

2. **SCOOP** about 30 seeds from one side of the pumpkin. Rinse them off and spread them out on paper towels to dry in a warm spot.

3. **FORM** the ground beef into a big patty.

4. **HEAT** the skillet on the stovetop over medium heat. Once the skillet is hot, add enough oil to coat the bottom of the pan and then add the patty.

5. **COOK** the patty well on the first side, about 8 minutes. The longer you cook the patty, the less chance it will break when you flip it.

6. To **FLIP** the burger, place the platter upside down on top of the skillet, then quickly flip the pan over and **PLOP** the patty onto the platter. You'll need oven mitts.

7. **RETURN** the skillet to the stovetop and add some more oil. Slide the patty off the platter and into the pan and cook until done, about 6 minutes.

8 When the burger is done, **PLACE** the platter on the pan and flip your burger onto the platter. See, it works! You just learned how to cook an enormous hamburger patty.

9 **ASSEMBLE** your burger, adding your toppings of choice and using the pumpkin halves as the bun.

10 For maximum effect, **GLUE** the diried pumpkin seeds onto the top half of the pumpkin like sesame seeds. Serve it up with a bottle of beer.

Beware: After sitting out on your front porch for a couple days, two and a half pounds of ground beef will start to rot. It also may attract a variety of uninvited varmints. If you're the crafty type and the thrill of displaying a real, supersized burger on your front lawn doesn't outweigh the drawbacks, you can fabricate your burger and toppings. For the patty, I recommend cutting a nasty old brown rug into a disc. For the tomatoes, cheese, lettuce, and other favorite burger toppings, use brightly colored felt cut into the appropriate shapes. If you don't like these suggestions, maybe you can think of something more convincing. I never claimed to be a Martha Stewart clone.

JUICY FACTS
EVERY BURGER LOVER NEEDS TO KNOW

- Though the origin of the burger is still up for grabs, three U.S. cities claim bragging rights: Seymour, Wisconsin; Hamburg, New York; and New Haven, Connecticut.

- Before the 1920s, "hamburger steaks" were served on toast or plain sliced bread.

- Founded in 1921, White Castle is the oldest hamburger chain. Today, burgers account for 40 percent of all sandwiches sold.

- A White Castle burger contains $1/18$ pound (25 g) of meat; a McDonald's burger contains $1/10$ pound (45 g); and a Burger King burger contains the most meat, $1/8$ pound (56 g).

- Denny's Beer Barrel Pub in Clearfield, Pennsylvania, offers a six-pound (2.75 kg) hamburger. Nineteen-year-old college student Kate Stelnick was the first person to have eaten it all within Denny's three-hour time limit. She weighs 115 pounds (52 kg).

- I like my burgers with no onions, no mayo, and extra pickles. My favorite burger is from the Fly Trap restaurant in Ferndale, Michigan. I want to marry Kate Stelnick and hold our reception at the Fly Trap, but my wife nixed that plan.

PUKING PUMPKIN

SO GROSS IT'S BECOME AN UNDERGROUND CLASSIC, THE PUKING PUMPKIN IS ALWAYS A FAVORITE OF VISITORS TO MY WEBSITE. To create the puke, I simply scooped some pulp through the pumpkin's big mouth. Lots of kids vomit on Halloween night, sickened by the combination of tons of candy and uncontrollable excitement. Lots of adults puke on Halloween, too, but from other sorts of more questionable combinations. Really, the Puking Pumpkin is emblematic of the entire holiday. Here's how to make your own in four easy steps.

Ga, Ga, Ga, Gaaaccckkk!

YOU'LL NEED

- **1 pumpkin shaped like a fat human head** (any size will do)

- **A doormat or scrap of old carpet** (optional)

- **CARVING AND GUTTING TOOLS: jigsaw, steak knife, big metal spoon**

  NOTE: Power tools are optional. (See The Standard Toolbox: Alternatives to Power Tools, page 7.)

(1) **SELECT** a good spot to display your pumpkin and do your carving there, as puke (pumpkin or otherwise) is not easy to transport. Alternatively, carve your pumpkin on a doormat; a shag carpet mat would look especially gross.

(2) **SCALP** the pumpkin and **REMOVE** about half of the guts.

(3) **CARVE** the eyes and nose. **ADD** a big, gaping mouth. **CLEAN** the rough edges.

(4) **PULL** some guts out of the mouth and place them in front of the pumpkin. You can leave a little pulp in the mouth and some dripping from the nose for effect.

(5) Go **DRINK** a beer or **EAT** some candy. You are done.

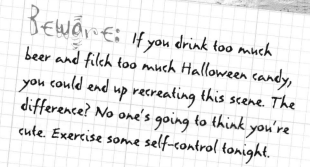

PUKING PUMPKIN

THEMES AND VARIATIONS

The theme of barfing offers endless opportunities for entertainment.

1) **BARFING BABY PUMPKIN:** Position a tiny pumpkin so it's puking on a larger pumpkin. Porch steps would work well for this scenario.

2) **BARF-BAG PUMPKIN:** Position a Puking Pumpkin so it's puking into a container, such as a brown paper bag or a discarded toilet or sink.

3) **BOOZING PUMPKIN:** Place an empty bottle of cheap whiskey next to a Puking Pumpkin.

4) **SHAME-ON-YOU PUMPKINS:** Surround a Puking Pumpkin with a number of smaller pumpkins wearing disgusted looks on their faces.

5) **PROM QUEEN PUMPKIN:** Position a glittering tiara next to a Puking Pumpkin with an otherwise pretty face.

6) **CHUNKY PUKING PUMPKIN:** Add candy bits or pieces of food to the pumpkin guts. A can of chili makes it look gross; so do strained peas.

BEWARE: If you drink too much beer and filch too much Halloween candy, you could end up recreating this scene. The difference? No one's going to think you're cute. Exercise some self-control tonight.

WORM-INFESTED PUMPKIN

THIS PUMPKIN DESIGN COMBINES MY LOVE OF
the fishing aisle at the local discount store with my desire to make everyone hurl. Inspiration struck while I was shopping for lures. "These fake worms would look cool wriggling out of a pumpkin's head," I thought. Then, while deciding what color worms to buy, I noticed that the store also stocked artificial maggots, mealworms, and other icky creepy-crawlies. Pay dirt!

*The worms crawl in,
the worms crawl out,
the maggots
play pinochle on
your snout.*

YOU'LL NEED

- **1 cute, round pumpkin** *(1 to 1½ times the size of a human head)*

- **CARVING AND GUTTING TOOLS: jigsaw, reciprocating saw** *(if pumpkin flesh is tough)*, **steak knife, big metal spoon**

  NOTE: Power tools are optional. *(See The Standard Toolbox: Alternatives to Power Tools, page 7.)*

- **Electric drill**

- **A selection of plastic worms and/or maggots from the fishing section of your favorite mega-store**

1. **SCALP** your pumpkin.

2. **SCRAPE** the inside walls to remove all the guts. You can roast the pumpkin seeds if you want (see page 61). Yum.

3. **CARVE** a scared-looking face. **CLEAN** the rough edges.

4. **DRILL** or **CARVE** some 3/8-inch (1 cm) holes into the pumpkin.

5. **INSERT** a plastic worm or two into each hole. You want it to look like the worms are eating the pumpkin flesh. To make it grosser, you can **ADD** some fake maggots; they should be sticky enough to attach without glue.

REVOLTING FACTS ABOUT DEATH

YOU MAY NOT WANT TO KNOW

I'm going to write about how the human body decomposes after death, and you're going to continue reading. You know you will. No matter how gross or uncomfortable it gets. I love you for that.

- After you die, the parts of your body die at different rates. Brain cells last three to seven minutes without oxygen, while skin can be removed and grow normally in a lab twenty-four hours after you are dead.

- Bodies decompose fastest in the air, second fastest in the water, and slowest deep in the ground.

- Even in a sealed environment where there are no worms, the microbes inside your body will start to eat you from within. The pancreas is often the first part of the body to digest itself.

- The gases created while your body decomposes often turn skin a green-blue color with blisters.

- In temperate environments, you will start to stink to the high heavens in four to six days. Much sooner in the tropics and later in cold climates.

- Above ground, a corpse will be rapidly broken down by insects and animals. In the tropics, maggots can engulf a corpse in twenty-four hours.

ENTHRALLING BOOKS ABOUT DEATH

YOU WON'T BE ABLE TO RESIST READING

If you couldn't stop yourself from reading every last horrifying detail above, then you will probably take morbid pleasure in the following books.

- *Being Dead: A Novel* by Jim Crace.

- *Cemetery Stories: Haunted Graveyards, Embalming Secrets, and the Life of a Corpse After Death* by Katherine Ramsland.

- *How We Die: Reflections on Life's Final Chapter* by Sherwin B. Nuland.

- *Stiff: The Curious Lives of Human Cadavers* by Mary Roach.

- *The Undertaking: Life Studies from the Dismal Trade* by Thomas Lynch.

- *What Happens When You Die: From Your Last Breath to the First Spadeful* by Robert T. Hatch.

MOLDY BEARD PUMPKIN

THIS PUMPKIN WILL GIVE MOST PEOPLE THE SUREFIRE HEEBIE-JEEBIES, and it's gnarly enough to send clean-freaks to Wretchinville. But the true beauty of this design lies in its passivity: just carve your pumpkin and let nature take its course. Of course, the Moldy Beard Pumpkin grows best in warmer climates, but even cold places like my hometown of Detroit will work. If you live in the South, carve it two weeks before Halloween. If you live in the North, three to four weeks beforehand should do. If you live in Alaska, start carving on Memorial Day weekend.

If This Reminds You of the Inside of Your Fridge, Stop Reading This Book and Start Fumigating

YOU'LL NEED

- **Dry erase marker**

- **1 pumpkin at least as large as a human head**
  (I prefer a tall, non-symmetrical face for this design)

- **A plastic tray or scrap of plywood**
  (you'll want to be able to move the pumpkin even after it turns into a warm, mushy pile)

- **CARVING AND GUTTING TOOLS: jigsaw, reciprocating saw** (if pumpkin flesh is tough), **router** (to shave off pumpkin skin), **steak knife, big metal spoon**

  NOTE: Power tools are optional.
  (See The Standard Toolbox: Alternatives to Power Tools, page 7.)

- **Spotlight** (optional)

Beware: If you neglect to place this pumpkin on a tray or another sturdy base before the mold begins to accumulate, you will live to regret it. Not only will it be impossible to display your Moldy Beard Pumpkin on your porch, it'll be revolting to transfer it into a garbage bag. Avoid this situation at all costs.

1. **DRAW** eyes and a mouth on the pumpkin. I think you are going for a homeless-person sort of expression. Be sure to include a beard in your sketch.

2. **SCALP** and **GUT** the pumpkin.

3. **CUT OUT** the eyes.

4. **SHAVE** the skin where you want the beard to grow. A rough texture in this area will encourage more mold growth, so don't shave too carefully.

5. **PLACE** the pumpkin on the base and leave it in a spot with lots of fresh air and a little sunlight. Molds need moisture and lots of fresh air to grow. Fortunately, the pumpkin will supply its own moisture. Try to keep it away from bugs if possible, but in my opinion, a few maggots add impact.

6. On Halloween, **DISPLAY** the pumpkin someplace where its decay can be examined in detail. I suggest a spot where contact is unavoidable, such as right by your front door.

7. You may want to **ILLUMINATE** the pumpkin with a spotlight. Use enough lighting to reveal that the growth really is mold.

CREEPY FACTS

ABOUT MOLDS AND FUNGI

- Molds and fungi are everywhere, both indoors and outdoors. **In fact, there are more than 100,000 species and scientists classify mold as a separate kingdom, distinct from both plants and animals. (Don't ask me which molds are growing on my Moldy Beard Pumpkin— I have no idea.)**

- You probably already know that penicillin was derived from a mold called *Penicillium*. **Some common fungi you may have encountered are apple-scab, corn smut, and wheat rust. Suffering from athlete's foot or jock itch? Both may be caused by mold, among other factors.**

- Don't worry: **most common molds are not hazardous to healthy people. However, too much exposure may cause or worsen conditions like asthma, hay fever, or other allergies.**

- Mold likes moisture. **That's why it grows in kitchens, bathrooms, and on slimy surfaces like carved and gutted jack-o'-lanterns.**

- Some fungi are yummy. **For example, people eat many kinds of mushrooms. Yeast is used in the fermentation of wine and beer (mmm, beer) and to make breads rise. And every time you order take-out Chinese food you eat a fungus called shoyu in your soy sauce.**

DROWNING-IN-A-BAG
PUMPKIN

SOME FOLKS THINK DROWNING WOULD BE A PEACEFUL WAY TO DIE. I don't know if that is true. Certainly, if someone trapped you in a very large bag of water, you would find it to be quite traumatic. It's also quite traumatic when you visit the neighbors' house and they have a creepy-looking, drowning pumpkin on their porch. Here's how you can drown your own pumpkin without even the slightest bit of remorse. I promise: This design spooks everyone who sees it, whether they're afraid of the water or not.

Too Bad Gourdy Doesn't Know How to Swim

YOU'LL NEED

- **Dry erase marker**

- **1 pumpkin the size of a human head** *(or a little larger)*

- **CARVING AND GUTTING TOOLS: jigsaw, reciprocating saw** *(if pumpkin flesh is tough)*, **router** *(to shave off pumpkin skin)*, **steak knife, big metal spoon**

  NOTE: Power tools are optional. *(See The Standard Toolbox: Alternatives to Power Tools, page 7.)*

- **2 or 3 really large, very thick, clear plastic bags**

- **Garden hose or other water source**

- **Waterproof light source, such as glow sticks or a waterproof lantern**

- **10 to 15 feet** *(3 to 4.5 m)* **rope**

1. **DRAW** a panicked face on the pumpkin.

2. **SCALP** and **GUT** the pumpkin.

3. **CARVE** the face in the pumpkin. **CLEAN** the rough edges. **SHAVE** the pumpkin skin from the eyeballs if you want to exaggerate them.

4. Double- or triple-**BAG** the pumpkin.

5. **HOLD** the tops of the bags as you fill them with water. You might need an accomplice for this job.

6. **DROP** your light source inside your pumpkin. If you use glow sticks, be aware that they will float. Just jab them into the inside flesh of the pumpkin to keep them in position.

7. **WRAP** the rope around the neck of the bag and tie it off. Looping the rope around the bag eight to twelve times gives it a creepy, nooselike appearance.

8. Once everything is in place, **PEEL AWAY** the excess layers of plastic to reveal the horror of the Drowning Pumpkin.

YUMMY ROASTED PUMPKIN SEEDS

OR HOW TO TURN PUMPKIN GUTS INTO TOTALLY DELICIOUS SNACKS

After seeing pumpkins burned and drowned and otherwise mangled, you might say you're not really in the mood for a snack. But I suggest that you reconsider. After you've burned or drowned or mangled your pumpkin, you'll have lots of leftover pumpkin guts, and pumpkin guts contain pumpkin seeds, which are really yummy if you season and roast them. Imagine if everything in life were like that? If you dig a hole, you don't get to eat the dirt. If you reroof your house, you don't snack on the leftover shingles. But if you carve a pumpkin, you do get to eat the pumpkin seeds. So show some gratitude, all right?

YOU'LL NEED
- An oven
- A baking sheet and mixing bowl
- Pumpkin seeds
- Melted butter
- Salt or seasoning

1) Preheat the oven to 300°F (149°C).

2) Do a mediocre job of separating the goo and guts from the actual seeds. Don't rinse off all the goop; it makes the seeds taste good.

3) Place the seeds in a mixing bowl and add the melted butter: I use 1 tablespoon (15 g) for every 2 cups (228 g) seeds.

4) Add salt: I suggest 1 teaspoon salt for every 2 cups (228 g) seeds. Alternatively, add one of the seasoning mixes listed below.

5) Toss thoroughly to combine, then spread the pumpkin seeds on an ungreased baking sheet in a thin layer.

6) Roast the seeds until they are nice and toasty, about 30 minutes. Stir them after 15 minutes so the sides toast evenly.

7) Take them out, cool them, and serve them with beer (or soda for the minors among us).

VARIATIONS: TASTY SEASONING IDEAS
Add any of the following mixtures to 2 cups (228 g) seeds.

- SPICY GARLIC MIX: 1 tablespoon (8.4 g) garlic powder, 1 teaspoon (6 g) salt, and 1/2 teaspoon (.9 g) cayenne pepper

- SOUTHWESTERN MIX: 2 teaspoons (4.6 g) cumin, 1 teaspoon (2.8 g) garlic powder, 1 teaspoon (6 g) salt, and 1/2 teaspoon (.9 g) cayenne pepper

- CURRY MIX: 1 tablespoon (6.3 g) curry powder and 1 teaspoon (6 g) salt

- SWEET AND SPICY MIX: 1/4 cup (55 g) sugar, 1 teaspoon (6 g) salt, and 1/2 teaspoon (.9 g) cayenne pepper

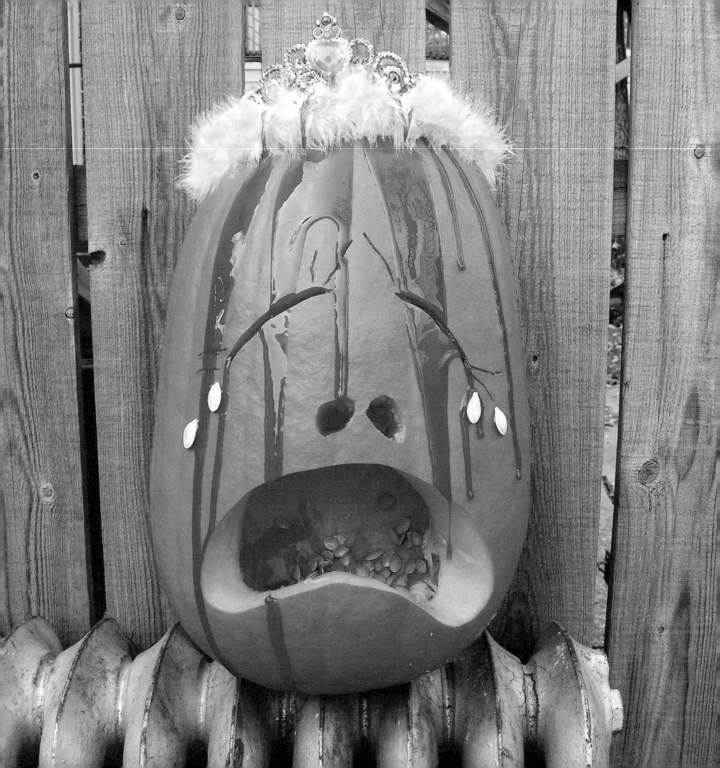

CARRIE PUMPKIN

IF YOU HAVE NEVER SEEN CARRIE, Brian De Palma's classic horror film based on Stephen King's first book, check it out this Halloween. Sissy Spacek plays Carrie White, a miserable social outcast who is bullied at home and at school. The culminating torment comes when her fellow students elect her prom queen in a rigged election. When she gets on stage, they dump buckets of pigs' blood on her head. But what none of the students realize is that Carrie has the power of telekinesis. She transforms from a mousy girl into a rage-filled monster and unleashes her own bloody revenge. This gruesome pumpkin immortalizes Carrie's cinematic turning point.

"It was bad, Mama. They laughed at me."
—CARRIE

1. **DRAW** a despondent face on the pumpkin with a huge wailing mouth. Try to imagine the expression you would make if your classmates elected you prom queen (or king) and then dumped buckets of pig's blood over your head.

2. **CARVE** the face and **GUT** the pumpkin through the mouth. **CLEAN** the rough edges. Save a few pumpkin seeds for tears.

3. **CROWN** the pumpkin with a tiara, **SET** in a pie plate, and **DRIZZLE** with fake blood.

4. **GLUE** the reserved pumpkin seeds on the pumpkin's cheek so they look like teardrops. How sad is that?

YOU'LL NEED

- **1 tall pumpkin** *(1 to 1½ times the size of a human head)*
- **Dry erase marker**
- **CARVING AND GUTTING TOOLS: jigsaw, steak knife, big metal spoon**

  NOTE: Power tools are optional. *(See The Standard Toolbox: Alternatives to Power Tools, page 7.)*
- **Tiara**
- **1 aluminum foil pie plate**
- **1 recipe fake blood** *(see page 10)*
- **Glue**

Variation:

Pump the blood over Carrie's face by attaching this pumpkin to a small Zen-style fountain. In step 3, instead of drizzling Carrie with fake blood, carve out the bottom of the pumpkin and position it in a roasting pan with the pump in its center. Drill some holes in Carrie's head: I suggest two points on her forehead (just under her tiara) and one at the top of her head. Poke the tubing through the holes and attach the other ends of the tube to the pump; you'll need two T-style connectors to join the tubes together. Darken some water with red food coloring, fill the pan with this mixture, and plug in the pump. The tiara and pumpkin seed teardrops complete the picture.

MORE CREEPY, CLASSIC HORROR MOVIES

IF YOU HAVEN'T SEEN THE FOLLOWING FLICKS, WHY NOT GIVE YOURSELF A GOOD SCARE THIS HALLOWEEN?

- **HENRY: PORTRAIT OF A SERIAL KILLER** (John McNaughton, 1986). No other movie will creep you out in a more realistic way than this movie, based on the life of a real serial killer, Henry Lee Lucas. Some movies scare you for the two hours that you are in the theater. This flatly displayed, unglamorous movie will scare you for the rest of your life.

- **THE EXORCIST** (William Friedkin, 1973). Very rarely does a horror movie manage to attract a mainstream audience during its opening. *The Exorcist* did, and all of those nonhorror spectators were fainting in their seats.

- **HELLRAISER** (Clive Barker, 1987). Horror movies can get kind of boring. *Hellraiser* introduces new characters and scenarios to keep you completely frightened.

- **THE SHINING** (Stanley Kubrick, 1980). Jack Nicholson can be a real American badass, and I love him for that. Here he is in all his glory: crazy, over-the-top, and terrifying.

- **PSYCHO** (Alfred Hitchcock, 1960). Speaking of badasses, I give you two words: Alfred Hitchcock.This film featured only one famous actress, Janet Leigh, and Hitchcock threw the audience for a loop by killing her in the very beginning. How badass is that? Her death scene is a piece of must-see cinematic history.

- **HALLOWEEN** (John Carpenter, 1978). Okay, this is the only movie on this list that resembles a standard horror movie: The sexy girls all die, the boyfriends all die, and the last heroine is the hardest to kill. But just try watching it at night with the sound up and the lights off. I guarantee you'll be scared out of your mind.

- **THE TEXAS CHAIN SAW MASSACRE** (Tobe Hooper, 1974). A crazy guy hacks things (and people) apart with power tools. Hmmm. Is it any wonder why I like this one? I could audition for any sequels.

- **A NIGHTMARE ON ELM STREET** (Wes Craven, 1984). Freddy Krueger is the scariest villain ever. Period.

- **EVIL DEAD II** (Sam Raimi, 1987). This is one of the few horror movies that I've seen in the theater. The high-speed motion of the movie is completely lost on a small TV, but if you have a bitchin' home theater, move this movie up to number two, after the bone-chilling *Henry*. Seriously. It's that good.

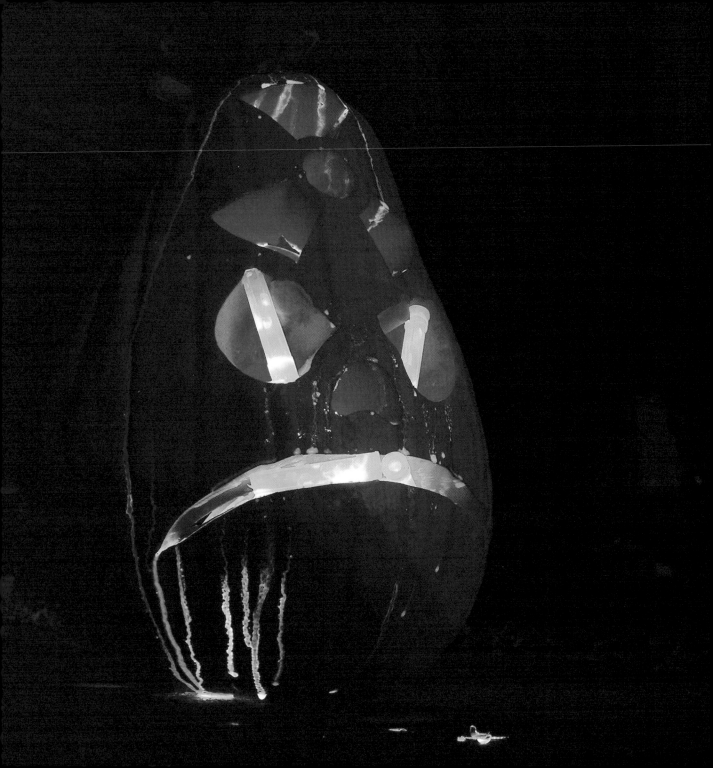

RADIOACTIVE PUMPKIN

LAST TIME I CHECKED, RADIOACTIVE STUFF DOESN'T ALWAYS GLOW. In fact, I think it only glows on watch faces and in B movies. On the other hand, people who nitpick details like that are pretty nerdy, so let's agree to ignore them. In the interest of complete transparency, I will admit this design has a few shortcomings. For maximum dazzle, it must be displayed in a warm, dark spot; fail to deliver these conditions and it will fizzle real fast. Choose a cozy bay window, turn off all the lights, and you should receive satisfactorily freaked-out reactions from everyone who passes by.

Stage a Meltdown in Your Front Yard

1. **SCALP** and **GUT** the pumpkin.
2. **DRAW** and **CARVE** a face that looks like it is in agony. **CLEAN** the rough edges.
3. **CRACK** the glow sticks and **SHAKE** them up about 10 minutes before you want to stage your meltdown.
4. **ARRANGE** the glow sticks in your pumpkin; **SLICE** a few of them open so the glow goo drips down the pumpkin's face. Display your radioactive jack-o'-lantern in a warm, dark place where it'll have maximum impact, like a living room window.

YOU'LL NEED

- **1 slightly pear-shaped pumpkin at least the size of a human head** (that way, it sort of looks like the radiation has caused a hideous brain tumor)

- **CARVING AND GUTTING TOOLS: jigsaw, reciprocating saw** (if pumpkin flesh is tough), **steak knife, big metal spoon**

  NOTE: Power tools are optional. (See The Standard Toolbox: Alternatives to Power Tools, page 7.)

- **6 to 8 small glow sticks or 3 to 4 large ones** (if you have the cash, buy more)

- **Heavy-duty pair of scissors**

Beware: Choose glow sticks that are labeled "nontoxic," please. For easy clean up, display your Radioactive Pumpkin on a cookie sheet wrapped in aluminum foil or other sturdy base.

THE SECRET LIFE OF GLOW STICKS

PLUS COOL THINGS YOU CAN DO WITH THEM

Ever wondered what makes glow sticks glow? My research reveals they contain two chemicals that are separated by a glass vial. The first chemical, phenyl oxalate ester (sometimes called by its brand name Cyalume), makes up most of the liquid inside the plastic stick. The small glass vial contains hydrogen peroxide. When you bend the stick, it breaks the glass vial and the phenyl oxalate ester mixes with the hydrogen peroxide. This creates a chemical reaction that causes the glow you see. As if that isn't enough fun, the manufacturers of glow sticks put various dyes inside the sticks so the light varies in color from stick to stick. After you've staged your Halloween meltdown, here are some fun things you can do with your leftover glow sticks.

- Freak out your neighbors by making a glow stick UFO: Simply attach glow sticks to a kite, activate them, and launch the mother ship.

- A bathtub filled with water, dry ice, and glow sticks is a cool way to keep beer cold.

- Sink glow sticks in the hot tub for a super-groovy 1970s effect.

- Put activated glow sticks in the punch bowl for an equally groovy effect. Lower the lights and your guests will be drawn to the bowl like magic.

- You can make Jell-O with a glow stick inside it, but you'll have to somehow activate the glow stick right when the party begins. Just remember to wash your hands before you fish around in the bowl of Jell-O, okay?

- Place glow sticks along your front sidewalk, driveway, or a trail in the woods to create an eerie entrance.

- If you need to find a gas leak, a glow stick is a great method to light the way. (Although past gas leaks at my house were always caused by the dog eating broccoli.)

CRIME SCENE PUMPKIN

HOLLYWOOD FILMMAKERS DON'T SEEM TO FULLY UNDERSTAND THE VISUAL POWER OF THE EXIT WOUND. This leads movie viewers to think bullets do most of their damage on the way in, when it's really the other way around. In my Crime Scene design, I've exaggerated the exit wound for maximum impact. With half the side of its head blown away, scattered pumpkin guts, and fake blood, this extreme pumpkin is as graphic as a John Woo film. Here's how you can create your own macabre crime scene.

The jig is up, jack.

1. **SELECT** a good spot to display your pumpkin and do your carving there. Alternatively, place your pumpkin on a piece of cardboard or a black plastic trash bag. This will help contain the carnage.

2. **SCALP** your pumpkin by cutting a circle around the stem and popping off the top.

3. **GUT** the pumpkin, scraping the inside walls to remove all the seeds and pulp. Reserve guts for later use.

4. **CUT** a frightened-looking face on the pumpkin. Next, **CUT** a multipointed, irregular-shaped star on one side of the pumpkin's head. That's your exit wound.

5. **BUST** the reserved pumpkin guts into smaller, randomly shaped pieces.

6. **BREAK UP** the cauliflower into chunks of various sizes. These will be the brains.

7. **MIX** the pumpkin guts and cauliflower chunks with the fake blood. **SCATTER** on the ground near the exit wound.

8. **DRIBBLE** some fake blood so it looks like it's running out of one corner of the pumpkin's mouth. Everyone knows that's the universal symbol for death by violence.

YOU'LL NEED

- **A piece of cardboard or a black plastic trash bag taped down at the corners** *(optional)*

- **1 pumpkin the size and shape of a human head** *(or a bit larger)*

- **CARVING AND GUTTING TOOLS: jigsaw, reciprocating saw** *(if pumpkin flesh is tough)*, **router** *(to shave off pumpkin skin)*, **steak knife, big metal spoon**

  NOTE: Power tools are optional. *(See The Standard Toolbox: Alternatives to Power Tools, page 7.)*

- **Sledgehammer**

- **Fake blood** *(see page 10 for recipe)*

- **1 head cauliflower**

NINE ALTERNATIVE USES

FOR FAKE BLOOD ON HALLOWEEN

1) **ADORABLE ROADKILL:** Buy an old and dirty but realistic-looking stuffed animal at a thrift store. Arrange its mangled body next to a driveway or roadside and cover liberally with fake blood. Tire marks leading away from the road kill will lend authenticity to the scene.

2) **"OUT, DAMNED SPOT!":** Soak old clothes in fake blood until they are saturated. Artfully position bloody handprints on a tattered sheet. Hang the soiled items from your clothesline. For verisimilitude, consider placing your weapon of choice nearby.

3) **SCARECROW MASSACRE:** Find or make a scarecrow for the sole purpose of maiming it. Scatter its innards, head, and bits of torn clothing over your front lawn. Top with plenty of fake blood.

4) **BLOOD SPRINGS ETERNAL:** Fill a tabletop fountain with fake blood instead of water.

5) **OPEN WOUND:** Mix shredded toilet paper with Vaseline and apply the concoction to your skin to create the illusion of a pus-filled wound. Add fake blood to make it look like it's dripping with gore.

6) **DEATH SCENE:** To recreate a death scene from your favorite kung fu movie, apply a little fake blood to your mouth so it drips out of one corner. If you swallow some in the process, don't worry— my recipe is completely edible.

7) **KILLER PANCAKES:** Substitute maple syrup for the corn syrup in the fake blood recipe. (Don't worry it's just sugar, cornstarch, and food coloring). Serve on pancakes.

8) **JELL-O BRAINS:** Jell-O molds come in all shapes and sizes. Luckily for us, some lost soul created a brain-shaped one. Add raspberry flavoring to the fake blood and pour over the Jell-O brain. Pineapple or lemon Jell-O is a good choice.

Beware: Like any crime scene, this one'll eventually get sticky and start to attract flies. That's why I always cleanse my crime scenes with a power washer. First, I scoop what remains of my victim (including any incriminating guts and blood-covered pulp) into a heavy-duty trash bag, which I deposit in a nearby trash can or Dumpster. Next, I mop the area with a powerful detergent and, finally, blast away any remaining stickiness with my power washer. It's like your pumpkin massacre never happened.

SKULL PUMPKIN

MY NINE-YEAR-OLD NEIGHBOR JACK asked if I'd help him carve a really cool pumpkin. He liked the idea of doing a creepy skull. I happened to have a pear-shaped pumpkin sitting in my driveway, so we got to work. We used a wood plane to shave off most of the pumpkin skin and some aluminum foil to doll up one of the front teeth. It took only ten minutes from concept to completion, and everyone thought the results were eerie.

Feeling Okay? You look a little pale...

YOU'LL NEED

- **1 pear-shaped pumpkin at least as large as a human head** *(narrower on top than the bottom)*

- **CARVING AND GUTTING TOOLS: jigsaw, reciprocating saw** *(if pumpkin flesh is tough),* **router** *(to shave off pumpkin skin),* **steak knife, big metal spoon**

  NOTE: Power tools are optional. *(See The Standard Toolbox: Alternatives to Power Tools, page 7.)*

- **Dry erase marker**

- **Large rasp, plane, angle grinder, or belt sander** *(to skin the pumpkin; any of them will do)*

- **Small piece of aluminum foil** *(use some left over from a sandwich; optional)*

1. **LOP OFF** the stem of the pumpkin to create a flat surface. **TURN** the pumpkin upside down so it is balanced where the stem used to be.

2. **CUT** a hole the size of your hand on the backside of the pumpkin. **INFORM** your nine-year-old neighbor that he needs to **CLEAN OUT** all the pumpkin guts or you'll tell Santa Claus he's been bad.

3. **DRAW** a skull face on the pumpkin; be sure to use a dry erase marker.

4. **CARVE** the face. Try to create bleak, hollow eyes for a genuinely skeletal appearance. **CLEAN** the rough edges. I **ROUTED** the teeth, too. Jack requested that I make it look like the skull didn't floss. I did my best.

5. **SKIN** the pumpkin using your tool of choice. I had a wood plane in the basement that I bought to fix a sticky door. Leave some streaks of pumpkin skin for contour.

6. **SPRAY** the pumpkin with a garden hose to remove all the shavings.

7. **CUT** eight legs extending from a hole in the cranium to create a cool spider logo.

8. **EMBELLISH** with a silver front tooth, if desired.

THE PSEUDOSCIENCE OF JACK-O'-LANTERNS

WHAT THE PERSONALITY OF YOUR PUMPKIN REVEALS ABOUT YOU

In the eighteenth and nineteenth centuries, some scientists thought much could be determined about a person's character and personality from the shape of his head. Hogwash, you say? Take a look at what I can tell about you by examining your jack-o'-lantern. Then we'll talk.

PUMPKIN CHARACTERISTIC	WHAT IT SAYS ABOUT YOU
Huge	You have too much self-esteem, and everyone is secretly jealous of you.
Teensy	You are always the one insisting that size doesn't matter.
Lopsided	You have considered plastic surgery but decided you wanted a flat-screen TV instead.
Dirty	You think cow manure and fresh air smell the same.
Shiny and clean	Trimming your fingernails is the closest you ever get to manual labor.
Rotten	You have dark secrets you've never shared with anyone.
Pimply	You have never known the mental anguish of an embarrassing blemish.
Very smooth	You are perfectly adequate.
Irregular	When you are in your sixties, your eyebrows will start to look like a row of shrubs.
Soft spot	The babysitter dropped you on your head when Mom wasn't looking.
Dented	You don't like pumpkin pie; you only eat it because you like Cool Whip.
Pear shaped	You believe fat-bottomed girls make the rocking world go round.
Fat on top, skinny on the bottom	You wouldn't make it in the Marine corps.
Tall and thin	You secretly desire to run for office.
Short and squat	You believe that pork is the other white meat. Bacon counts.

BLOOD-FILLED PUMPKIN

THIS PUMPKIN IS MORE THAN A COOL DESIGN; IT'S ALSO AN INGENIOUS PRANK. Imagine inviting your mother-in-law over to carve an innocent-looking pumpkin. She draws the face, and when she inserts her knife, blood starts oozing out of the eye socket or dripping from the side of its mouth. I guarantee, it'll be the highlight of your Halloween.

What's Halloween Without a Totally Revolting Prank or Two?

YOU'LL NEED

- **Lots of fake blood**
  (see page 10 for recipe)

- **Marinade injector**
  (In case you don't already
  know, this thing is basically
  a 9-inch [23 cm] syringe for
  meat. You can find an injector
  in any store that sells cooking
  accessories. This item is multi-
  functional, so don't worry about
  spending a few dollars on it. You can
  use it to carve a "needle-in-the-eye"
  pumpkin or to prepare a succulent
  turkey at Thanksgiving.)

- **1 small, cute, innocent-looking
  pumpkin** (about the size of a
  monkey's head)

- **Unsuspecting victim and/or
  bystanders**

- **PUMPKIN-CARVING-PARTY TOOLS:**
  **dry erase markers, jigsaw,
  steak knives, big metal spoons**

  NOTE: Power tools are optional.
  (See The Standard Toolbox:
  Alternatives to Power Tools, page 7.)

① **MIX UP** a large batch of fake blood. If your pumpkin is the same size as a monkey's head, tripling the recipe should do it.

② **PIERCE** the pumpkin with a freshly cleaned marinade injector. **NOTE:** Avoid piercing too close to the stem because that section of pumpkin flesh is difficult to puncture. In general, you want to pierce the pumpkin in an inconspicuous area.

③ **FILL** the marinade injector with fake blood and inject it into the pumpkin. Once you empty the injector, pull out its plunger and add more fake blood to the injector body while the needle stays in the pumpkin. Repeat until the pumpkin is full of blood. **NOTE:** Do not remove the needle from the pumpkin between batches; this will turn the hole red.

(4) Before you pull out the marinade injector, **PUT** a couple of tablespoons of water in it. As you pull the syringe out, **PUSH** the water through the needle. The water helps the hole "heal," concealing it from the innocent people you're trying to trick.

(5) **HOST** a pumpkin-carving party. Tell guests that you will supply the pumpkins. Reserve the Blood-Filled Pumpkin for your favorite unsuspecting friend or relative.

(6) **SIT BACK** and enjoy the spectacle as your prissy sister-in-law's Mickey Mouse pumpkin starts oozing blood out of its eye socket.

CARAMEL ONION, ANYONE?

Whip up a batch of these caramel onions masquerading as caramel apples. Unlike some Halloween pranks, this one is almost completely harmless. Plus, you'll enjoy the fact that your greediest friend will certainly be the first to grab an "apple" and sink his teeth in.

YOU'LL NEED
- **4 to 6 apple-sized onions, peeled**
- **A caramel apple kit:** *usually includes the caramel wraps and the sticks. Sprinkles, mini marshmallows, crushed nuts (all optional)*
- **Waxed paper**

1) Follow the directions on the kit, substituting onions for apples. If you chose your onion size properly and completely cover them with the caramel, it will be almost impossible to tell the difference.

2) If you want to make your caramel onions look extra delicious, decorate them with sprinkles, marshmallows, or crushed nuts.

3) Arrange the "apples" on waxed paper so the caramel and toppings won't stick. Serve and watch the fun unfold.

SATANIC PUMPKIN

I AM CERTAIN IT WAS MY BELIEF IN SATAN that got me this book deal. The proof? Although my degree in engineering guarantees that I can't write a single intelligible sentence, courtesy of Satan, I have an editor who corrects all the rubbish I write. How cool is that? I know at least thirty God-fearing English majors who've never published a word. As thanks to the Prince of Darkness, I plan to carve this jack-o'-lantern every year. If you want a book deal, luxury car, or TV show of your own, consider creating a Satanic Pumpkin for your front porch this Halloween.

YOU'LL NEED

- **1 pumpkin** (twice the size of a human head)

- **A pair of parsnips** (those yucky-tasting white carrots that God created for some reason; consider them another motivation to join Satan's team)

- **1 long red chili pepper**

- **CARVING AND GUTTING TOOLS: jigsaw, reciprocating saw** (if pumpkin flesh is tough), **router** (to shave off pumpkin skin), **steak knife, big metal spoon**

NOTE: Power tools are optional. (See The Standard Toolbox: Alternatives to Power Tools, page 7.)

FOR THE KEROSENE FIRE:

- **Bucket**

- **Kerosene** (available at the hardware store and even some gas stations)

- **Roll of toilet paper**

- **Long lighter or long kitchen matches**

- **Fire extinguisher** (type A-B or A-B-C)

"Halloween Is My Holiday!"

1 **SCALP** your pumpkin by cutting a circle around the stem and popping off the top.

2 **GUT** your pumpkin, scraping the inside walls to remove all the pulp and seeds.

3 **CARVE** a devilish face, including some nasty fangs. **CLEAN** the rough edges. To make the fangs look yellowish, **SHAVE** off the pumpkin skin to reveal the flesh beneath.

4 **CUT** two holes in the top of the pumpkin where you want Satan's horns to sprout. Make the holes a tad smaller than the parsnips at their largest point.

5 **PUSH** the parsnips through the holes from the inside of the pumpkin until they are snugly stuck in the holes. (This is the coolest; most people think the parsnips enter from the outside of the pumpkin.)

6 **NAIL** or **GLUE** the stem end of the chili pepper inside the mouth to give Satan a Gene Simmons–like tongue.

7 What's Satan without some fire and brimstone? For long-lasting towering flames, I recommend that you **USE** the kerosene to light your pumpkin. (If you'd prefer to use charcoal lighter fluid and newspaper, see pages 20–21 for instructions.)

 8 **CUT** a few vent holes (each about 2 inches [5 cm] wide) in the backside of the pumpkin about one-third of the way up. These vents will feed air to the fire.

9 **SOAK** the roll of toilet paper in the kerosene until it's completely saturated, at least 30 minutes.

 10 **STICK** the entire roll of kerosene-soaked toilet paper into the pumpkin cavity. There should be air space surrounding it.

11 To avoid bodily harm, **IGNITE** the toilet paper through the mouth opening. If you light it from the top or with a short match, you are likely to experience hellfire firsthand. Don't say I didn't warn you.

12 **KEEP** your cell phone handy because Hollywood is about to call. (Your concerned neighbors might, too.)

BEWARE: Do not light up this (or any) jack-o'-lantern inside your home—or without adult supervision. Satanic flames belong in an open outdoor area, far away from anything flammable. If your lawn is dry, spray it down with the hose before you light the pumpkin. Always keep your fire extinguisher handy.

DEVILISH PRANKS

THE STORY OF THE JACK-O'-LANTERN

An old Irish legend tells the tale of Stingy Jack, a mean bastard who loved to play tricks on everyone: friends, family, his mother. Even the Devil himself.

One Day, Stingy Jack tricked the Devil into climbing an apple tree. Once the Devil was up there, Jack put crosses all around its trunk. The Devil was stuck. In exchange for letting the Devil down, Jack made him promise never to take his soul to Hell.

When Jack died, Saint Peter barred him from Heaven, and the Devil had already promised not to let him into Hell. Instead, the Devil placed an ember from the fires of Hell inside a hollowed out turnip and handed it to Jack to light his way back up to earth. From that day onward, Jack wandered the earth with his "jack-o'-lantern."

Pumpkins are larger and easier to carve than turnips, so in the late 1800s, Irish immigrants to the United States updated the tradition and made their jack-o'-lanterns out of pumpkins.

CONJOINED TWINS
PUMPKIN

CONJOINED TWINS HAVE ALWAYS CAPTIVATED US.

We wonder what it would be like if even our most intimate moments were witnessed by a twin we couldn't escape. But if you think about it, nature has always created such couplings. What gardener hasn't come across a giant green pepper (or tomato or potato or apple) that, on closer examination, turns out to be not one, but two joined veggies or fruits? To create a convincingly conjoined jack-o'-lantern, you don't need to search the pumpkin patch. Turn the page for a few cheap tricks instead.

Two heads are better than one, especially if they're attached.

YOU'LL NEED

- **2 pumpkins of approximately the same size and shape**
  (I recommend ones that are much larger than a human head)

- **Dry erase marker**

- **CARVING AND GUTTING TOOLS: jigsaw, handsaw, steak knife, big metal spoon**

  NOTE: Power tools are optional.
  (See The Standard Toolbox: Alternatives to Power Tools, page 7.)

- **Electric drill and twine** *(optional)*

- **Candles or a flashlight**

1. **DRAW** the pumpkins' big, stupid grins. The wider the smiles, the better. Don't make the faces exactly identical, just weirdly similar looking.

2. **CARVE** the faces and **GUT** the pumpkins through the orifices.

3. **ARRANGE** the pumpkins side-by-side on the same flat surface.

4. **HACK** matching vertical slices from the side of each pumpkin so there's a gaping hole in the side of each pumpkin. If you need to draw a template on each pumpkin before you saw, that's okay, but estimating works fine, too.

5. **PUSH** the cut sides of the pumpkins together.

6. If you need to **ADJUST** your pumpkins so that they look more convincingly conjoined, you can do one of three things:

   a) **SHIM** the bottom of the pumpkins so that they line up better.

   b) **STITCH** the back of the pumpkins together using a drill and some twine.

   c) **RECUT** one of the pumpkins.

7. **DISPLAY** the pumpkins on your porch, choosing an angle that makes your twins look convincingly conjoined. Illuminate with candles or a flashlight. (Okay, I'll admit this design is kind of a cheap trick. But when you see the Conjoined Quintuplets Pumpkin I'm planning for next year, you'll definitely be impressed.)

CHANG AND ENG

The most famous conjoined twins were Chang and Eng, born in Thailand (then called Siam) in 1811. In 1829, they traveled to the U.S. where they married two women, fathered twenty-one children, and lived to be more than sixty years old. They are responsible for the term "Siamese twins," which is not medically accurate, so it is rarely used. Not all twins from Thailand are attached to their siblings; not all conjoined twins are from Thailand. Got it?

MOONING PUMPKIN

WHY ARE KIDS RESPONSIBLE FOR MOST RANDOM ACTS OF MOONING? Popular wisdom suggests it's because they are prone to doing stupid things, which—like mooning—involve acting before they think. I would like to offer a different theory: As we age, our butts look worse and worse. By the time you're my age, society wants you to keep that ugly, saggy thing covered up, and so do you. In fact, at this point, the prospect of mooning other people seems like something that would embarrass me more than them. If you're past the first blush of youth but still want to moon a friend or enemy, why not spare yourself the humiliation and put a Mooning Pumpkin on their front lawn instead?

Show Your Neighbors a Little (Dis)Respect

YOU'LL NEED

- **Jigsaw**

  NOTE: Power tools are optional. *(See The Standard Toolbox: Alternatives to Power Tools, page 7.)*

- **10 feet** *(3 m)* **of 2 x 2-inch** *(5 x 5 cm)* **lumber**

- **2 matching pumpkins, each the size of an ample butt cheek**

- **Deck screws and screwdriver**

- **Electric drill and 2¹/₂-inch** *(6 cm)* **hole saw attachment**

- **Set of clothes, including pants, shirt, and shoes**

- **Sledgehammer**

- **Dried leaves or newspaper**

- **Staple gun**

1. **SAW** the lumber into two 40-inch (1 m) pieces, one 14-inch (35 cm) piece, and one 13-inch (32 cm) piece.

2. **SHARPEN** one end of each of the 40-inch (1 m) stakes. These will be the legs of your mooning pumpkin.

3. Eight inches (20 cm) from the top of the 40-inch (1 m) stakes, **SCREW** in the 13-inch (32 cm) piece to form a crossbar. Use deck screws to secure the connection. Six inches (15 cm) further down, screw in the 14-inch (35 cm) piece to form a second crossbar. Think of these two pieces as the pelvis: They will keep the pumpkins from sliding down the legs.

4. **DRILL** holes through the heels of the shoes. This will allow you to put the stakes through them.

5. **FIT** the pants over the stakes.

6. **DRILL** a hole in the bottom of each pumpkin. The top of the stakes will be shoved into these holes to put the butt cheeks in position.

7. **STUFF** the shirt with old newspaper or leaves.

8. In the dead of the night, **SNEAK** over to your friend's house. When you get there:

a) **ARRANGE** the pants and shoes on each stake and **DRIVE** the stakes into the ground so a full moon will shine on your friend's front door. A hammer may be necessary.

b) **STICK** the pumpkins on the stakes.

c) **POSITION** the pants at the bottom of the pumpkins; **ATTACH** them to the pumpkin using the staple gun.

d) **STAPLE** the bottom of the shirt to the top of the pumpkins.

e) **LET** the shirt fall forward. This should give the illusion of a fully bent-over, mooning person.

9. **SNEAK HOME** and wait 365 days for your friend to take his revenge.

Consider pairing your Mooning Pumpkin with this trashy Trucker Lady, inspired by the mud flap art of a dirty, old tractor-trailer. Yee-haw!

FIVE CRUDE THINGS

YOU'LL WISH YOU NEVER LEARNED ABOUT MOONING

1) One of the first reported incidents of mooning was in 1346 during the Battle of Crécy, when several hundred Norman soldiers mooned the English archers.

2) Since 1979, people in Laguna Niguel, California, spend an entire Saturday in July mooning the passing Amtrak trains. If you think this is some form of protest, you are incorrect. It all began as a dare at a nearby bar. See www.moonamtrak.org for details.

3) When you moon someone out a window and put your naked buttocks against the glass it is popularly referred to as a "pressed ham."

4) Mooning someone while spreading your butt cheeks may be called giving them the red-eye, the brown-eye, or even the stink-eye.

5) According to my friend Dane, if you stand on your chair in a crowded place and moon in four separate directions, it is called "doing a lighthouse." If you do perform a lighthouse, let's hope that no one blows a foghorn.

INDEX

After a hard afternoon of pumpkin carving, there's nothing like enjoying a cold beer with your buddies.

ACKNOWLEDGMENTS

I would like to thank my wife, Lisa. Never has the question "What does she see in him?" been asked so often. I owe my parents and siblings a big thanks for allowing me to develop into a subversive yet successful person. I would like to thank my drinking buddy Matt for helping me execute some of my more volatile creations and for always being willing to light the match (or fuse). Rob Cockerham of www.cockeyed.com is an important inspiration. His idea that pranks can be harmless and completely victimless deserves fame and success.

Thanks to Marian Lizzi for discovering me and my website and to Penguin for publishing my book. I am happy we made this book together, although it is too bad we couldn't agree to print it on gasoline-infused paper like I requested. Tons of thanks to Quirk Packaging, the team that had to deal with me on a daily basis. Sarah Scheffel, my editor, must have a gigantic brain or own some type of high-tech scanning device because she managed to turn the manuscript that I wrote on hamburger wrappers into this book. Also, Lynne Yeamans created the design that transformed this book from a nut job's manifesto on pumpkins into a fun family read. I am sure there are many other people to thank at Perigee and Quirk but smart managers have learned to keep me away from anyone who works hard.

Finally, I would like to thank the unknown guy who wandered around my childhood neighborhood dressed in a gorilla suit, scaring the crap out of my friends and me.

THE EXTREME PUMPKIN CHALLENGE
WHO CAN CARVE THE MOST GRUESOME PUMPKIN OF THEM ALL?

Every year I post my favorite new pumpkin designs on my website: www.extremepumpkins.com. If you have a truly horrific (or hilarious or otherwise outrageous) design and would like to win an admittedly terrible prize, visit the site and e-mail us a photo. You might want to check out past winners for inspiration. **SOME OF THEM ARE BADASS.**

ABOUT THE AUTHOR

TOM NARDONE is the founder of ExtremePumpkins.com, an alternative pumpkin-carving website with a large and largely deranged following. He is the founder of PriveCo, the world's most private company. Evenings and weekends, you'll find him in his garage creating lunatic projects to delight his children and horrify his wife. He lives in the suburbs of Detroit with three happy kids and the aforementioned long-suffering bride, Lisa.